Contents

How to use this book

Each page has a title. It tells you what the page is about.

I tell you what to do here. Read it very carefully before you start.

Sometimes there is a 'Hint' to help you.

Each question has a number.

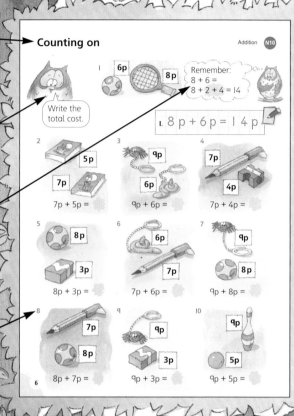

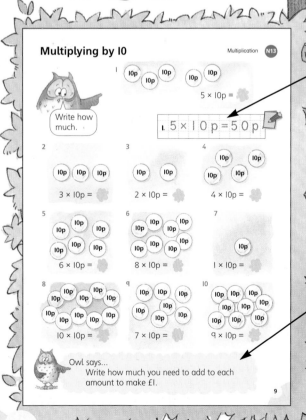

Write the work in your book like this. The first one is always done for you.

I sometimes ask you to do a bit more work. Put the answers in your exercise book.

Read these problems very carefully.

Taking away

Write the new prices.

3p off

17p

17p – 3p =

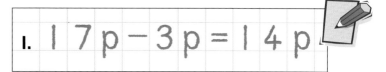

1. $17p - 3p = 14p$

2

15p

1p off

15p – 1p =

3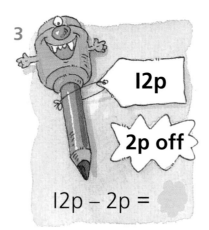

12p

2p off

12p – 2p =

4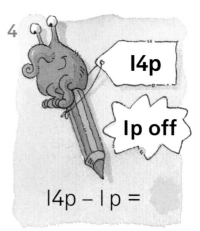

14p

1p off

14p – 1p =

5

16p

4p off

16p – 4p =

6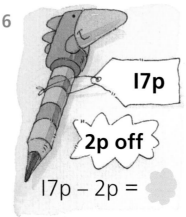

17p

2p off

17p – 2p =

7

13p

2p off

13p – 2p =

8

15p

3p off

15p – 3p =

9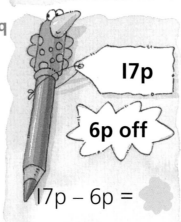

17p

6p off

17p – 6p =

10

18p

5p off

18p – 5p =

Adding 10

Write the new total.

I

$35 + 10 =$

I. $35 + 10 = 45$

2

24

$24 + 10 =$

3

43

$43 + 10 =$

4

52

$52 + 10 =$

5

38

$38 + 10 =$

6

75

$75 + 10 =$

7

46

$46 + 10 =$

8

67

$67 + 11 =$

q

55

$55 + 11 =$

10

37

$37 + 11 =$

Even and odd

Write the next 3 even numbers.

1  26

1. 28 30 32

2 42

3 34

4 28

5 18

6 48

7 36

8 20

9 52

10 30

Write the next 3 odd numbers.

1 33

1. 35 37 39

2 51

3 25

4 29

5 77

6 19

7 43

8 61

9 7

10 13

Counting on

Write the total cost.

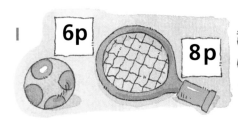 

6p **8p**

Remember:
8 + 6 =
8 + 2 + 4 = 14

I. 8 p + 6 p = 1 4 p

2

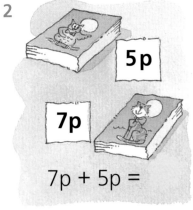

5p
7p

7p + 5p =

3

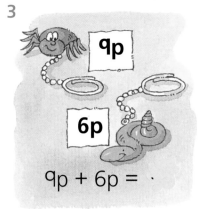

qp
6p

qp + 6p =

4

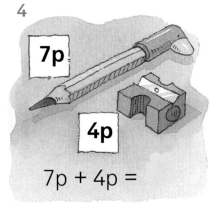

7p
4p

7p + 4p =

5

8p
3p

8p + 3p =

6

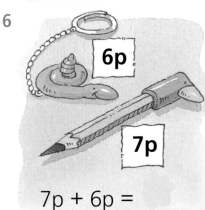

6p
7p

7p + 6p =

7

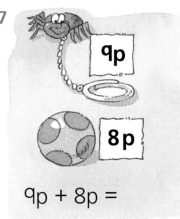

qp
8p

qp + 8p =

8

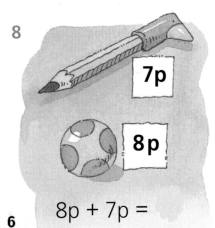

7p
8p

8p + 7p =

q

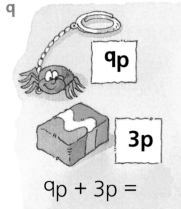

qp
3p

qp + 3p =

10

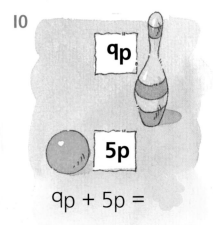

qp
5p

qp + 5p =

Buying

1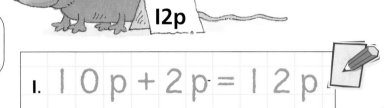
12p

Write the fewest coins needed to buy each toy.

1. 10p + 2p = 12p

2
16p

3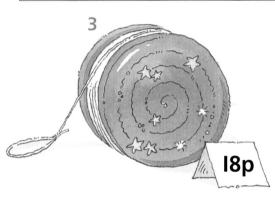
18p

4
23p

5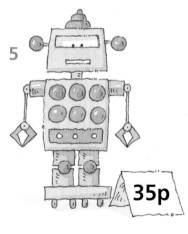
35p

6
32p

7
27p

Multiplying by 2

Write how many shoes.

1   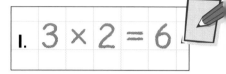   3 × 2 =

1. 3 × 2 = 6

2

6 × 2 =

3

8 × 2 =

4
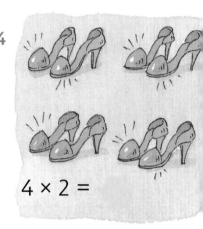
4 × 2 =

5

1 × 2 =

6
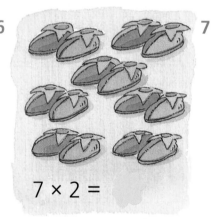
7 × 2 =

7
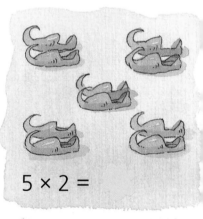
5 × 2 =

8
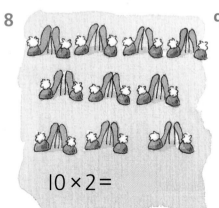
10 × 2 =

9

2 × 2 =

10
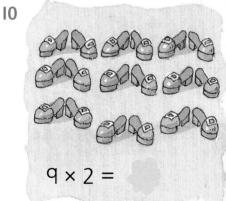
9 × 2 =

Multiplying by 10

Write how much.

1.
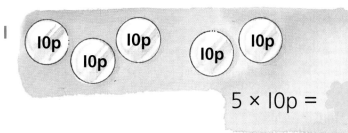

$5 \times 10p =$

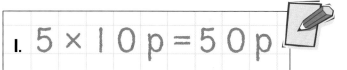

1. $5 \times 10p = 50p$

2.

$3 \times 10p =$

3.
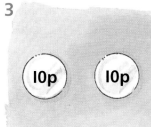

$2 \times 10p =$

4.
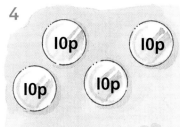

$4 \times 10p =$

5.
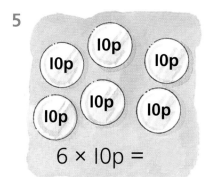

$6 \times 10p =$

6.

$8 \times 10p =$

7.

$1 \times 10p =$

8.
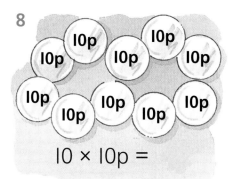

$10 \times 10p =$

9.
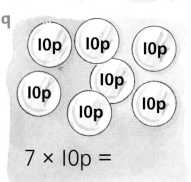

$7 \times 10p =$

10.
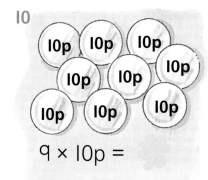

$9 \times 10p =$

Owl says...
Write how much you need to add to each amount to make £1.

Tens and units

Copy, then write the missing numbers.

1

$$40 + \boxed{} = 46$$

1. $40 + 6 = 46$

2

$$20 + \boxed{} = 23$$

3

$$30 + 5 = \boxed{}$$

4

$$70 + \boxed{} = 71$$

5

$$\boxed{} + 4 = 64$$

6

$$80 + 2 = \boxed{}$$

7

$$\boxed{} + 5 = 55$$

8

$$90 + \boxed{} = 97$$

9

$$30 + \boxed{} = 33$$

10

$$\boxed{} + 6 = 86$$

11

$$60 + 7 = \boxed{}$$

12

$$\boxed{} + 5 = 95$$

13

$$30 + 7 = \boxed{}$$

Owl says...
Use cards to make some other tens and units numbers between 20 and 50.

Doubling

Write the cost of two.

7p

1 7p + 7p =

1. 7 p + 7 p = 1 4 p

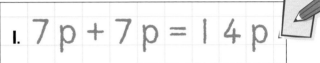

8p

2 8p + 8p =

10p

3 10p + 10p =

6p

4 6p + 6p =

3p

5 3p + 3p =

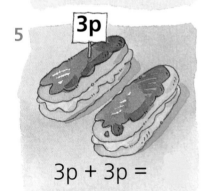

4p

6 4p + 4p =

1p

7 1p + 1p =

9p

8 9p + 9p =

5p

9 5p + 5p =

2p

10 2p + 2p =

Owl says...
Start with 1. Double it. Double the new number. Keep going.

Addition pairs

Write an addition
to match each strip.

I

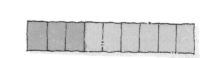

I. $3 + 6 = 9$

2

3

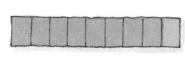

4

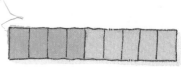

5

6

7

8

q

10

II

12

13

Owl says...
Use cubes to make patterns for eight.
Write the additions.

Subtracting 10

10 apples fall down.
How many are left?

27

27 – 10 =

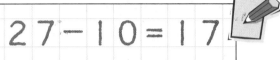

I. $27 - 10 = 17$

2

36

36 – 10 =

3

46

46 – 10 =

4

84

84 – 10 =

5

34

34 – 10 =

6

31

31 – 10 =

7

55

55 – 10 =

8

30

30 – 10 =

q

78

78 – 10 =

10

40

40 – 10 =

Owl says...
Subtract 11 from each answer.

Counting in 3s, 4s and 5s

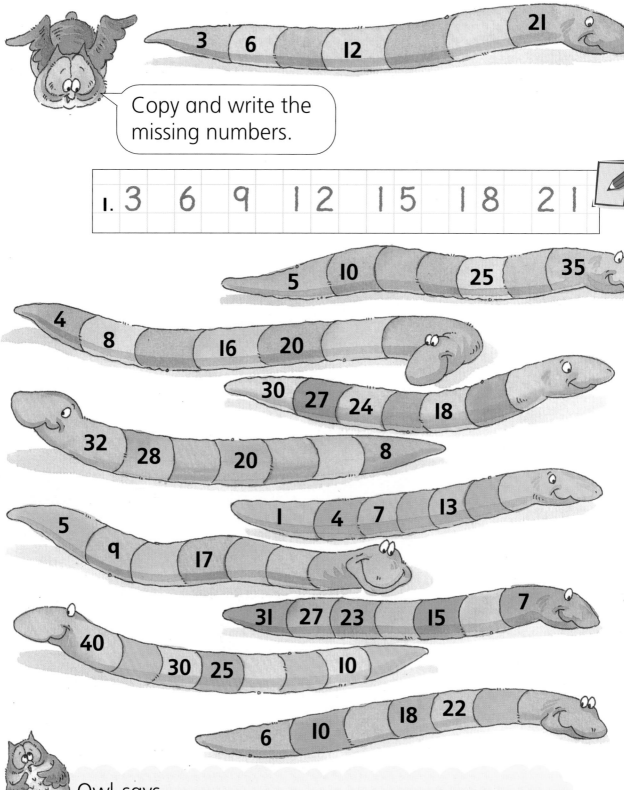

Copy and write the missing numbers.

1. 3 6 9 12 15 18 21

Owl says...
Draw some of your own snakes with missing numbers.

Adding or subtracting

Write the missing number.

I. $24 - 8 = 16$

1 $24 - 8 = $

2 $23 - 6 = $

3 $17 + = 22$

4 $22 - = 18$

5 $18 + 4 = $

6 $21 - = 16$

7 $ - 6 = 20$

Problems

8 Ben has **23 points**. He wins **4 points** but then loses **10**. How many now?

9 Ashleigh has **26 points**. She wins **3 points** but then loses **8**. How many now?

15

10 more, 10 less

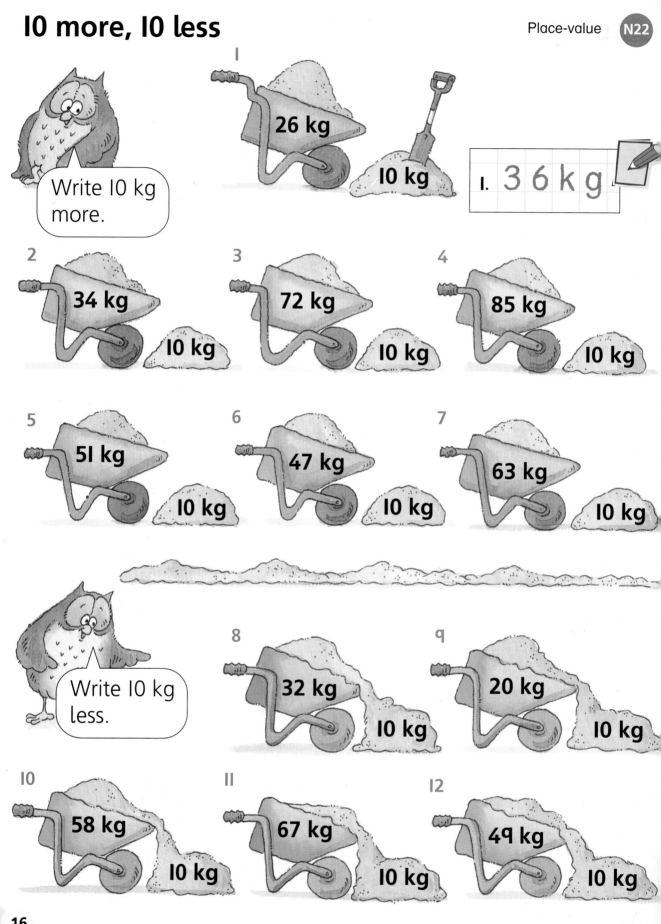

Write 10 kg more.

1. 26 kg 10 kg

1. 3 6 k g

2. 34 kg 10 kg

3. 72 kg 10 kg

4. 85 kg 10 kg

5. 51 kg 10 kg

6. 47 kg 10 kg

7. 63 kg 10 kg

Write 10 kg less.

8. 32 kg 10 kg

9. 20 kg 10 kg

10. 58 kg 10 kg

11. 67 kg 10 kg

12. 49 kg 10 kg

Adding

Write the new total.

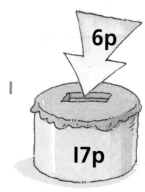

1.   17p + 6p =

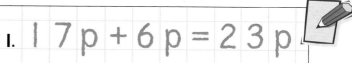

1.   1 7 p + 6 p = 2 3 p

2.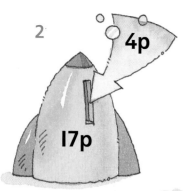

17p + 4p =

3.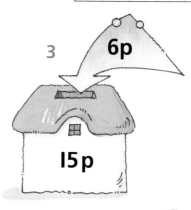

15p + 6p =

4.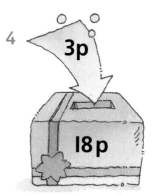

18p + 3p =

5.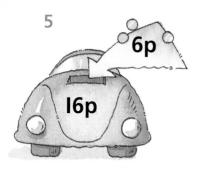

16p + 6p =

6.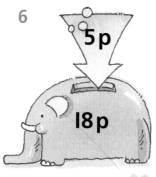

18p + 5p =

7.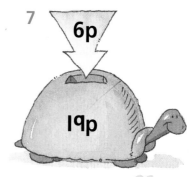

19p + 6p =

Problems

8.   Asseem has **16p**. She gets **8p** pocket money. How much now?

9.   Mark has **17p**. He gets **5p** pocket money. How much now?

Subtracting

Write how many are left.

1  $22 - 4 =$

1. $22 - 4 = 18$

2

$16 - 7 =$

3

$15 - 6 =$

4

$24 - 5 =$

5

$23 - 4 =$

6

$14 - 5 =$

7

$12 - 4 =$

8

$25 - 7 =$

9

$22 - 5 =$

10

$23 - 5 =$

Owl says...
Make up 5 subtractions of your own with an answer of 15.

Multiplying by 5

How many arms?

1.  $3 \times 5 =$

1. $3 \times 5 = 15$

2

$5 \times 5 =$

3

$6 \times 5 =$

4

$2 \times 5 =$

5

$8 \times 5 =$

6

$7 \times 5 =$

7

$10 \times 5 =$

8

$4 \times 5 =$

9

$9 \times 5 =$

10

$1 \times 5 =$

Owl says...
Write how many arms if each starfish had 10 arms.

Dividing

Write a division.

1. $15 \div 3 = 5$

1

2

3

4

5

6

7

8

9

10

Ordering

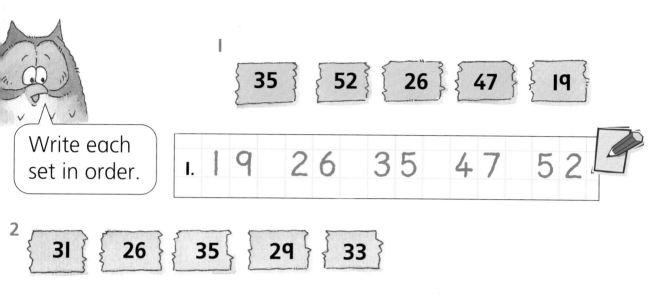

Write each set in order.

1.

| 35 | 52 | 26 | 47 | 19 |

I. 19   26   35   47   52

2.

| 31 | 26 | 35 | 29 | 33 |

3.

| 47 | 43 | 48 | 46 | 44 |

4.

| 15 | 31 | 19 | 42 | 23 |

5.

| 58 | 45 | 26 | 62 | 35 |

6.

| 24 | 39 | 42 | 40 | 30 |

7.

| 71 | 25 | 17 | 38 | 32 |

Owl says...
Write all the pink numbers in order.
Now do the blue, then the yellow numbers.

Adding 3 numbers

Choose 3 balloons.

Write an addition.

Write 10 additions using different balloons.

1. $8 + 2 + 6 = 16$

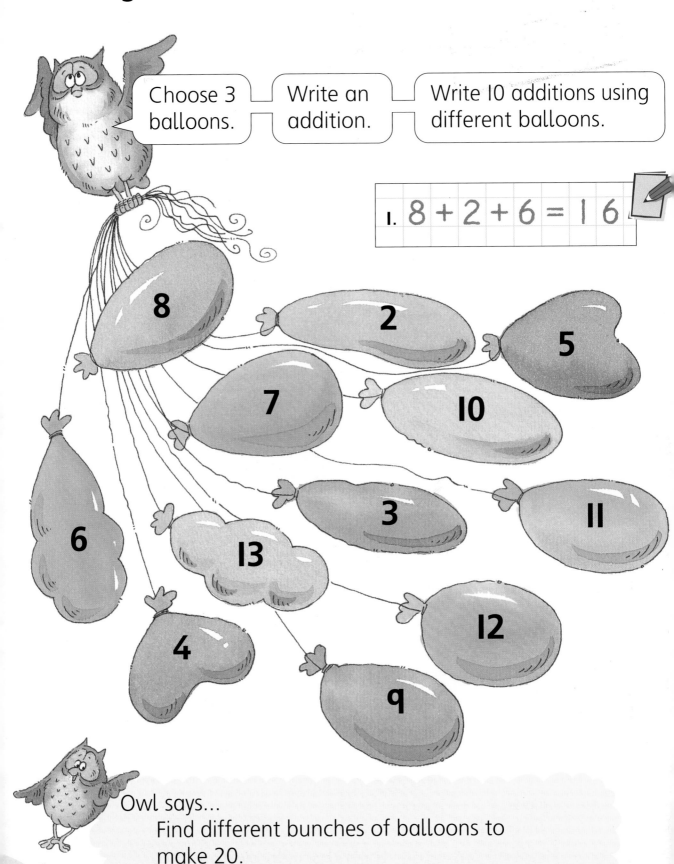

Owl says...
Find different bunches of balloons to make 20.

Addition pairs

Write the missing number.

1　15 +  = 20

I. $15 + 5 = 20$

2　 + 17 = 20

3　12 + = 20

4　 + 7 = 20

5　 + 2 = 20

6　4 + = 20

7　19 + = 20

8　40 + = 100

9　 + 30 = 100

10　 + 10 = 100

11　80 + = 100

12　60 + = 100

13　 + 50 = 100

 Owl says...
Draw pairs of cards that total 100.

55

45

Doubling

Luka runs to each cone... and back. How far is it?

1.

1. $30m \rightarrow 60m$

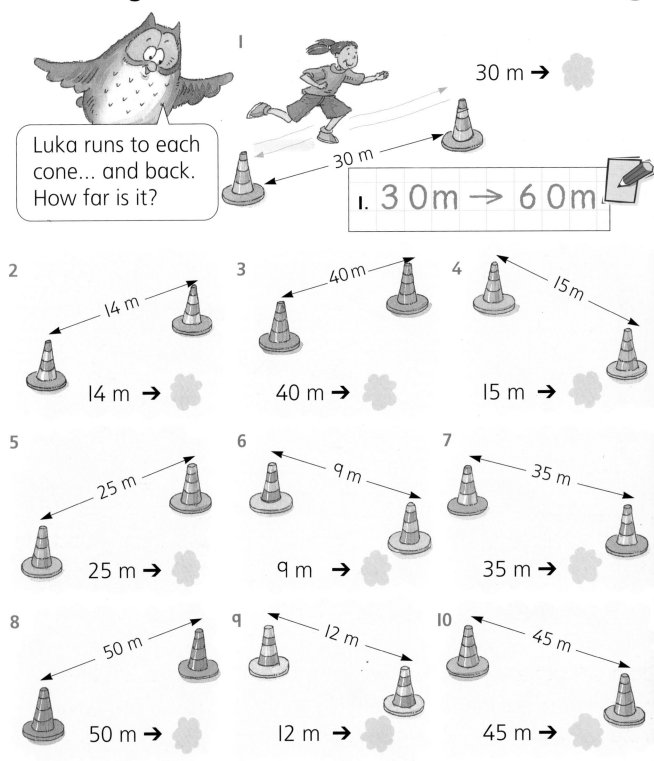

2. 14 m ➔

3. 40 m ➔

4. 15 m ➔

5. 25 m ➔

6. 9 m ➔

7. 35 m ➔

8. 50 m ➔

9. 12 m ➔

10. 45 m ➔

Owl says...
Draw some cones. Write the distance they are apart. Write how far there and back.

Difference

Write the difference between the race times.

I

43 min

47 min

I. 4 minutes

2

44 min

39 min

3

51 min

56 min

4

62 min

58 min

5

23 min

29 min

6

13 min

19 min

7

31 min

33 min

Problems

8

Jo has **9** more toy cars than Anu.

Anu has **27** cars.

How many cars does Jo have?

9

Kay walks to school in **18 minutes**.

Andy walks to school in **22 minutes**.

What is the difference in time?

10

Marka has **26p**.

Ali has **7p** more.

How much does Ali have?

25

I more, I less

Write I more and I less.

1

342

I. 3 4 1   3 4 2   3 4 3

2

462

3

100

4

210

5

666

6

533

7

371

8

244

9

718

10

895

Owl says...
Write 10 more and 10 less than each number.

Halving

Write half of each length.

I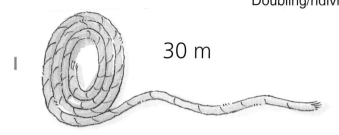

30 m

I. 30m → 15m

2

26 m

3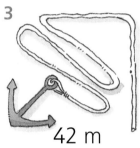

42 m

4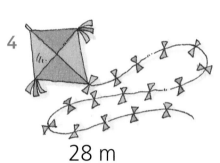

28 m

5

50 m

6

64 m

7

36 m

Problems

8

There are **32** children in class H.

Half are boys.

How many are girls?

9

Half of the girls have short hair.

How many girls in class H have long hair?

10

Class H drive **45 miles** to the seaside.

How far do they travel there and back?

Nearest 10

Write the length of each snake to the nearest 10 cm.

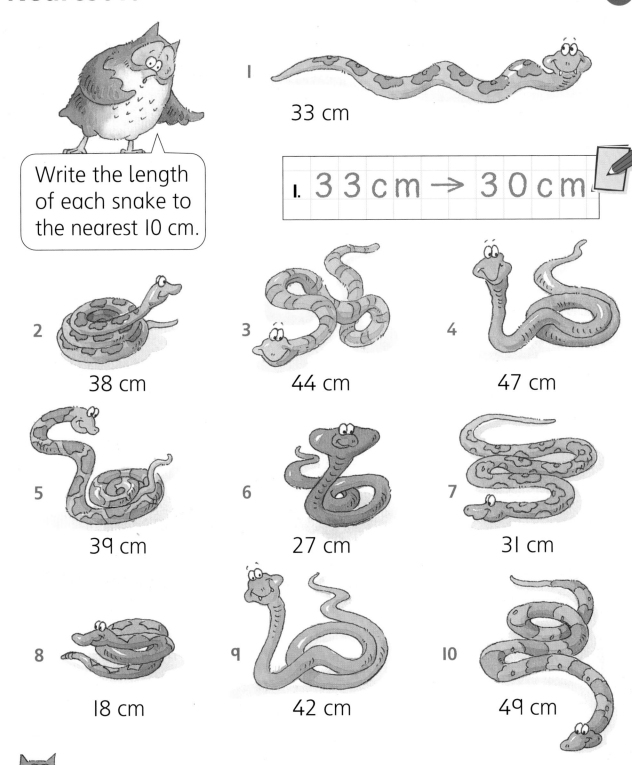

1 33 cm

1. 3 3 c m → 3 0 c m

2 38 cm

3 44 cm

4 47 cm

5 39 cm

6 27 cm

7 31 cm

8 18 cm

9 42 cm

10 49 cm

Owl says...
Each snake grows 10 cm. Write the new length and the nearest 10 cm.

How much change?

How much change from 30p?

1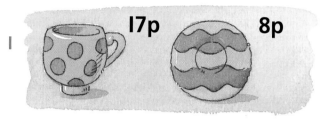

17p   8p

I. $17p + 8p = 25p$

$30p - 25p = 5p$

2
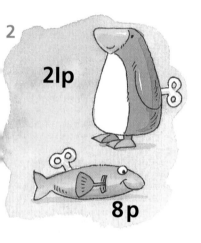
21p
8p

3

15p
12p

4
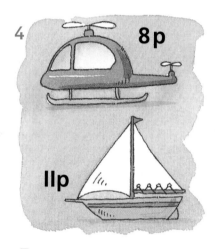
8p
11p

5

5p
19p

6

13p
9p

7

19p
5p

Owl says...
How much change from 50p each time?

Adding near doubles

How much do the bags weigh in total?

1.

5 kg   6 kg

I. $5\,kg + 6\,kg = 11\,kg$

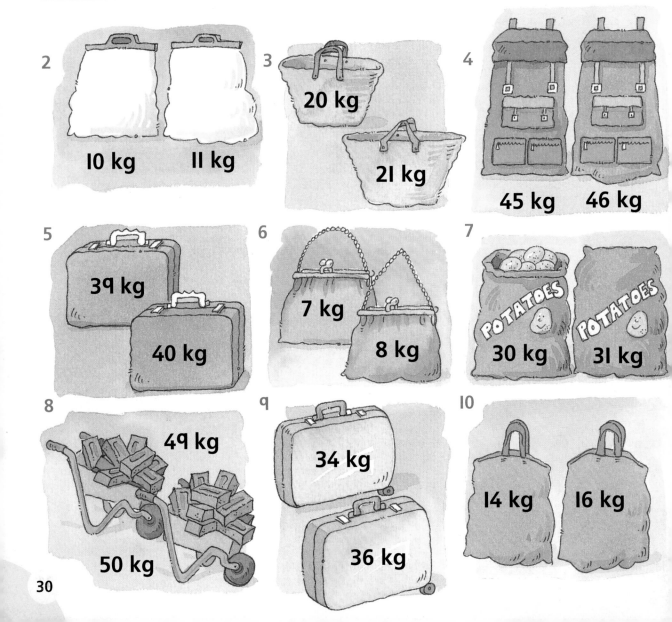

2
10 kg   11 kg

3
20 kg
21 kg

4
45 kg   46 kg

5
39 kg
40 kg

6
7 kg
8 kg

7
POTATOES
30 kg   POTATOES 31 kg

8
49 kg
50 kg

9
34 kg
36 kg

10
14 kg   16 kg

30

Multiplying

Write a multiplication for each egg box.

1.  4 × 2 =

1. $4 \times 2 = 8$

2.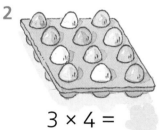

3 × 4 =

3.

2 × 2 =

4.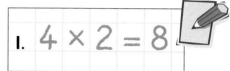

5 × 4 =

5.

3 × 3 =

6.

6 × 2 =

7.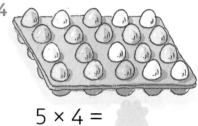

2 × 3 =

8.

5 × 5 =

9.

6 × 4 =

10.

5 × 3 =

Owl says...
Draw different egg boxes, each with 24 eggs in total.

Dividing

Write a division.

1

1. $12 \div 4 = 3$

2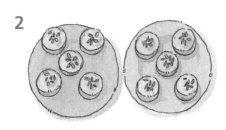

3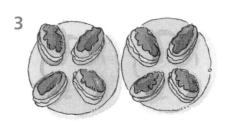

4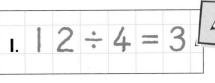

5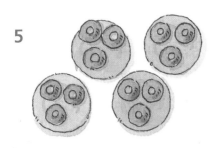

6

7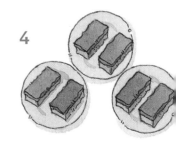

8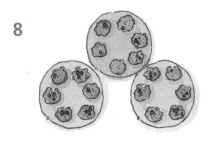

9

10

Owl says...
You have 18 cakes. How many different ways
can you group them equally?